Nature's Fury
LIGHTNING

John Hamilton

ABDO
& Daughters

VISIT US AT
WWW.ABDOPUB.COM

Published by ABDO Publishing Company, 4940 Viking Drive, Suite 622, Edina, Minnesota 55435.
Copyright ©2006 by Abdo Consulting Group, Inc. International copyrights reserved in all countries.
No part of this book may be reproduced in any form without written permission from the publisher.
ABDO & Daughters™ is a trademark and logo of ABDO Publishing Company.

Printed in the United States.

Editor: Paul Joseph

Graphic Design: John Hamilton

Cover Design: Neil Klinepier

Cover Photo: Corbis

Interior Photos and Illustrations: AP/Wide World Photos, p. 4, 7, 10

Corbis, p. 15, 16, 18, 21, 23, 25, 27, 28, 29

Digital Stock, p. 1, 3, 11, 14

John Hamilton, p. 17

Mary Evans Picture Library, p. 6

Photospin, p. 5, 9, 12-13

NASA, p. 19 (bottom)

NOAA, p. 19 (top)

Library of Congress Cataloging-in-Publication Data

Hamilton, John, 1959–
      Lightning / John Hamilton.
         p. cm. — (Nature's fury)
         Includes index.
      ISBN 1-59679-332-5
      1. Lightning—Juvenile literature. 2. Atmospheric electricity—Juvenile literature. I. Title.

      QC966.5.H36 2005
      551.56'32—dc22
                                                              2005045293

CONTENTS

A SHOCKING KILLER

ON JUNE 13, 1991, 40,000 GOLF FANS GATHERED AT HAZELTINE
National Golf Club in Chaska, Minnesota, to watch the U.S. Open Championship.
The day started warm, under a blue sky. Even though storms had been forecast, when
black clouds rolled in from the west it took most people by surprise.

The fast-developing storm shot
bolts of lightning through the air. Many
people fled to their cars or to nearby
buildings, but some stayed on the golf
course. Six men hid under the canopy
of a weeping willow tree about 30 feet
(9 m) tall. They
thought they'd be
safe because there
were so many taller
oak trees nearby.
But they made a
big mistake. It's a
myth that lightning
will always strike
the tallest object on the ground. Instead,
lightning searches for the *easiest* path
to the ground, and the rain-soaked,

electrically-charged canopy of the willow
tree made a perfect target.

The wind whipped up, and rain
poured from the sky. Suddenly, there
was a flash. The six men crumpled to
the ground like rag dolls. Some were
temporarily
paralyzed,
while others
were knocked
unconscious.
One man's heart
stopped beating—
he died from
cardiac arrest. The
tremendous voltage of the lightning bolt
caused his death, and there was nothing
paramedics could do to save him.

A Hazeltine lightning victim is
loaded into an ambulance.

Some scientists estimate that lightning strikes somewhere on the earth about 100 times each second. It can be a beautiful natural spectacle, but it is also extremely dangerous. Hurricanes, tornadoes, and floods get a lot of attention in newspapers and TV because of the tremendous mass destruction they can inflict all at once. Lightning, on the other hand, is an underrated killer because it strikes down only a few people at a time. But lightning is second only to flooding as the most dangerous weather-related killer in the United States. According to the U.S. government's National Oceanic and Atmospheric Administration (NOAA), lightning kills an average of 67 people each year in the United States. Reported injuries from lightning average about 300 per year. Lightning also causes hundreds of millions of dollars in damage to houses and other buildings, and is one of the main causes of forest fires.

Zeus holds lightning bolts as he rides his war eagle.

Lightning has always struck fear and wonder into people throughout history. It played a big part in myths, superstitions, and early religions. The ancient Greeks and Romans believed the god Zeus used lightning as a weapon. A place where lightning struck the ground was said to be holy, and temples were erected on the spot.

The Norse god Thor, like Zeus, used lightning to battle his enemies. Indra, from the ancient Hindu religion of India, was the god of thunderstorms. Navajo Indians of the American Southwest told tales of the mythical Thunderbird, who shot lightning bolts from its eyes. The Bantu tribes of Africa also worshiped a lightning bird-god.

Today we know that lightning is a discharge of static electricity in the atmosphere. It continues to fascinate people with its beauty. But those who fail to heed its danger often pay with their lives.

A barn, struck by lightning, continues to burn as a thunderstorm rages over the Indiana countryside.

THE SCIENCE OF LIGHTNING

LIGHTNING SOMETIMES STRIKES DURING VOLCANIC ERUPTIONS. It can also be found in intense forest fires and large explosions such as nuclear bombs. In rare cases lightning has even been observed during snowstorms. But the most common environment in which to find lightning is in the violent turmoil of a thunderstorm.

Thunderstorms occur in surprisingly large numbers. Scientists estimate that at any given moment, there are 1,800 storms rumbling overhead somewhere on the earth. On average, there are 16 million thunderstorms each year. Scientists use electronic devices to detect when lightning strikes. On average, there are 25 million strokes of lightning each year in the United States alone. That's a lot of lightning for scientists to study, but there is still much to learn about this mysterious force of nature.

Nobody is one hundred percent sure how lightning develops in a thunderstorm. The most accepted theory is that thunderstorms produce ice particles, which create friction. This friction causes giant pools of static electricity to form in the clouds.

Big thunderstorms are created when a weather system, such as a cold front, causes unstable air to rise rapidly in the atmosphere. Some thunderstorms create clouds that soar up to 60,000 feet (18,288 m), more than 11 miles (17.7 km) into the sky. Temperatures at that great height are very cold. When moisture in the air rises up inside the cloud, it turns to ice crystals.

Ice crystals are critical to forming lightning. If a cloud isn't high enough

Lightning strikes near a city. In the United States alone, 25 million strokes of lightning occur each year.

to produce ice crystals, it probably won't produce much, if any, lightning. In large thunderstorms, the ice crystals vary in size, from very small flakes to big hailstones. Air currents inside the cloud make the ice swirl around, pushing the ice up and down, rising and sinking with the winds. All this motion causes the crystals to rub and brush up against each other. These collisions in turn cause a separation of electrical charges, much like the static electricity caused by rubbing a comb on a piece of fabric.

Hail and ice crystals rub together inside clouds, creating electrical charges.

Light ice crystals with positive electrical charges rise to the top of thunderstorms, while negatively charged particles and hailstones swirl around towards the bottom of the clouds. This separation of negatively and positively charged particles creates an enormous potential for a violent electrical surge. This is called an *electrical differential*.

It is the potential energy that a cloud contains.

In addition to the electrical activity going on inside a thunderstorm, huge blobs of positively charged particles travel over the ground, following the storm as it blows across the landscape. Attracted by the vast pools of negative electrical energy in the bottom of the thunderstorm, these positive pools of energy tend to climb on tall objects such as trees and houses as they seek a way to connect with the thunderstorm. Sometimes when standing out in an open field in the middle of a thunderstorm, people can feel the hair on their heads stand up. This is because they are in a pool of positive electrical charge that is rising up. This is a very bad sign. If you cannot seek shelter, crouch down and stay away from trees. Lightning may be about to strike at any moment.

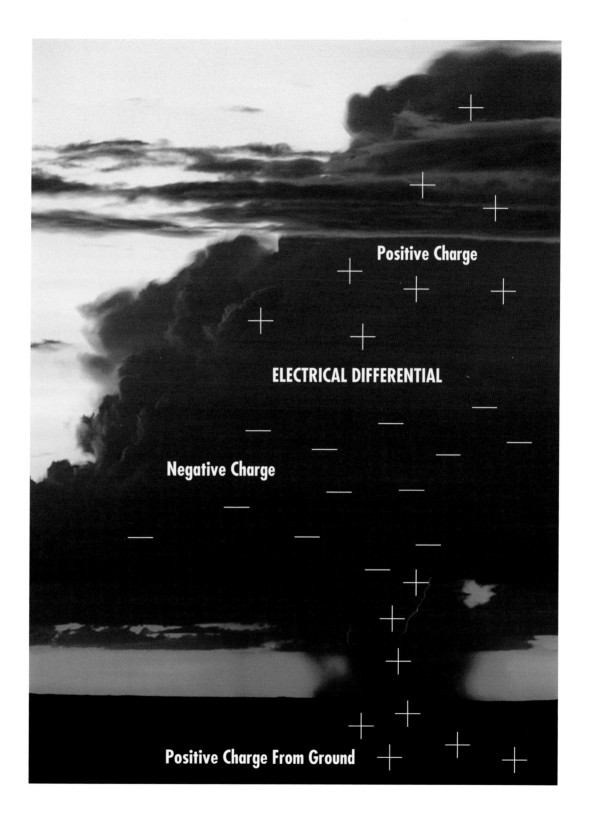

Cloud-to-ground lightning is the most dangerous kind of lightning. It begins when the electric charge in a cloud become very strong. Air around the cloud starts to break down and becomes *ionized*. This makes it easier for electricity to flow through the air.

When the conditions are just right, a streamer of electricity starts moving downward in a step-like motion, about 164 feet (50 m) at a time. This takes place in a fraction of a second. This streamer is called a *stepped leader*. As it grows it creates a channel through which electricity can flow.

As the stepped leader nears the earth, another streamer is launched up from the ground. It intercepts the stepped leader and creates a connecting path. A return stroke of electricity flies up the ionized air at nearly the speed of light. An enormous amount of energy is released, and a blinding white-blue flash of light is seen. Secondary strikes

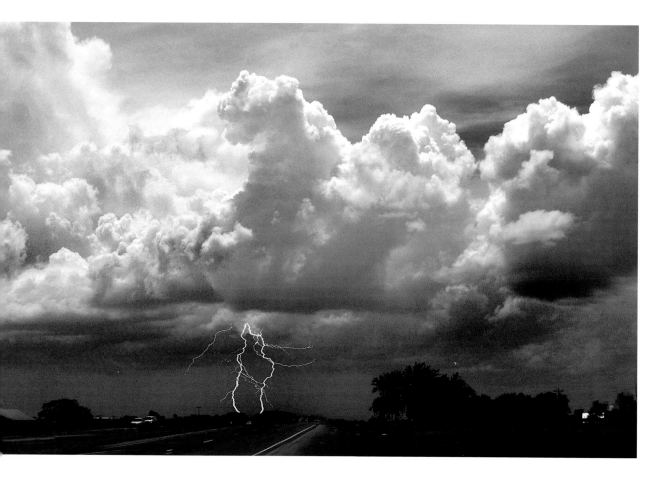

may occur as many as 40 times along the same path, all in a fraction of a second, traveling back and forth until the electrical potential is neutralized. We can see this as a flickering of the light, disproving the old saying that lightning never strikes the same place twice.

Because of all the energy in a lightning strike (usually involving several hundred million volts, with a peak current of 20,000 amperes), air around the electric current becomes superheated to 50,000 degrees F (27,760 degrees C), which is about five times hotter than the surface of the sun. The air is heated so quickly that it expands rapidly, exploding and causing a shockwave that travels outward. Thunder is the noise we hear created by the shockwave. If lightning strikes close enough, you can feel the shockwave as it passes by. The shockwave is powerful enough to damage buildings and injure people, but its force decreases with distance.

KINDS OF LIGHTNING

THE LIGHTNING THAT WE ARE MOST OFTEN AWARE OF IS CALLED cloud-to-ground lightning. This is what we think of as "normal" lightning. It is the most dangerous kind of lightning because people or buildings can be badly damaged. However, cloud-to-ground lightning accounts for only about 20 percent of all lightning strikes.

The most common type of lightning happens within a cloud. This is called *intra-cloud* lightning. These kind of electrical discharges happen between the two oppositely charged parts of a cloud. To somebody on the ground, it looks like the cloud is lighting up and flickering from within, although sometimes a bolt may shoot out of the cloud. Intra-cloud lightning is usually seen on hot, stormy nights when large thunderstorms roll across the landscape. Observed from a great distance, the tall thunderclouds seem to glow and flicker. It's an eerie sight, especially when you are so far away that you can't even hear the accompanying thunder.

Nobody knows why sometimes electrical discharges stay within a cloud, and sometimes they hit the ground. It probably has something to do with the strength of the electrical field in the bottom of the cloud. Also, clouds that develop great heights seem to have more intra-cloud lightning than cloud-to-ground lightning.

Less common but still as spectacular is *inter-cloud* lightning. This happens when electricity is discharged between two separate clouds. Aircraft and even

Cloud-to-ground lightning.

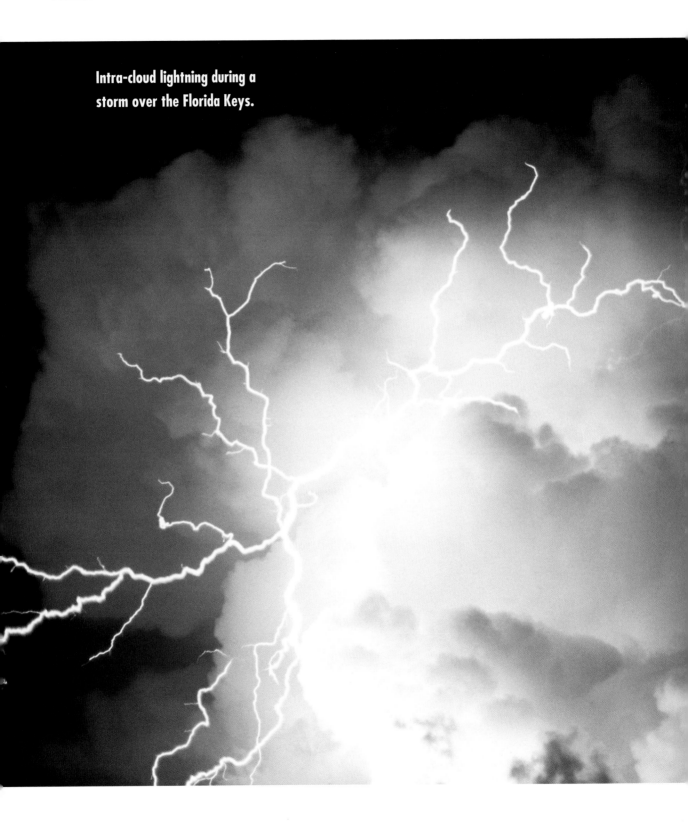

Intra-cloud lightning during a storm over the Florida Keys.

spacecraft, such as one of the Apollo missions, have been struck by intra-and inter-cloud lightning. Luckily, this kind of lightning, although more common, has only about one-tenth the energy of cloud-to-ground lightning.

There are many other names for the various kinds of lightning. *Sheet lightning* is another name for intra-cloud lightning, the stroke that happens inside a cloud, making it visible from many miles away. It is called sheet lightning when an observer is close enough to hear the thunder.

If you are too far away to hear thunder, but can still see the cloud light up, it is called *heat lightning*. It is called this because it is often observed on hot summer nights, when the overhead sky is clear but thunderstorms are observed at a great distance. Usually storms that are more than 10 miles (16 km) away are too distant for an observer to hear thunder. This distance varies, however, depending on air temperature and terrain. It's not unusual to hear distant thunder without actually seeing the storms producing them.

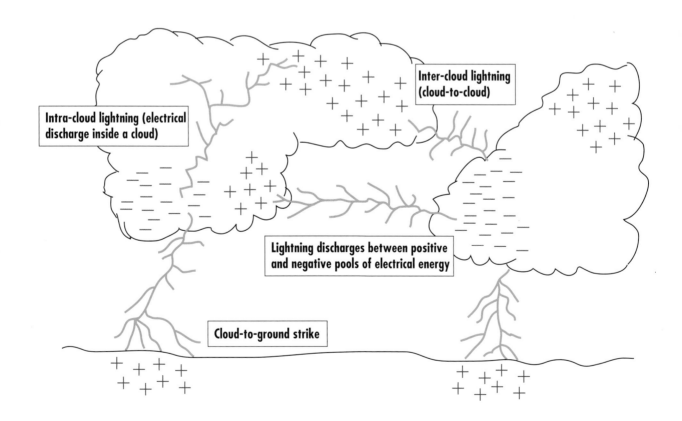

Intra-cloud lightning (electrical discharge inside a cloud)

Inter-cloud lightning (cloud-to-cloud)

Lightning discharges between positive and negative pools of electrical energy

Cloud-to-ground strike

Hot summer evenings sometimes produce heat lightning, which occurs when you can see clouds lit up by lightning strokes, but are too far away to hear thunder.

Forked lightning are the crooked branches you see during a typical lightning stroke. As the electric current tries to find the easiest path to release its energy, it sometimes sends out branches that don't quite make it all the way because of air resistance. These branches, however, also light up at the moment of discharge.

Ball lightning is extremely rare, and not well understood by scientists. These are glowing, phantom-like spheres about the size of a basketball. When they are seen, it is almost always after a very violent thunderstorm where much electrical activity has occurred. A lightning bolt is first seen hitting the ground, and then the ball lightning appears, hovering or slowly moving over the ground.

Ball lightning can last for just a few seconds, or even a few minutes. It has been witnessed on airplanes and ships, as well as in people's homes. Ball lightning doesn't seem to do much damage before it disappears, but it can leave behind burn marks when it travels through windows or screens.

A family is terrified by ball lightning floating through their home.

In recent years, scientists have discovered colored flashes of light that appear far above thunderstorms. They seem to be different kinds of lightning, which appear at the same moment regular lightning is discharged from a storm cloud. These high-altitude strikes occur in the middle and upper atmosphere. *Red sprites* are huge but weak flashes that look like carrot stems. *Blue jets* appear as small streaks shooting up from the tops of clouds. *Green elves* spread through the atmosphere and look like glowing jellyfish.

A video image of a red sprite, as seen from space.

FRANKLIN'S EXPERIMENT

BEFORE THE AGE OF SCIENCE, PEOPLE USED TO THINK THAT lightning was magic in the sky, or a sign of the gods. Even as late as the 18th century, what people believed about the natural world was more superstition than fact.

Ben Franklin, the famous American statesman and inventor, proved through scientific experiments that lightning was a form of electricity. This seems obvious to us today, but back then the biggest spark of electricity that people could make was only an inch or so long. It seemed likely that the enormous displays of thunderstorms were a different kind of force altogether, but Franklin set out to prove lightning and electricity were one and the same.

In June 1752, Franklin made a kite from a sturdy silk handkerchief. A wet string made of hemp was attached to the kite at one end, and to an iron key at the other. A silk ribbon, which doesn't conduct electricity as easily, was also attached to the key. Franklin held the ribbon as he flew the kite during a spring storm.

Joseph Priestley, a friend of Franklin's, later wrote, "The kite being raised, a considerable time elapsed before there was any appearance of its being electrified. One very promising cloud had passed over it without any effect; when, at length, just as he was beginning to despair of his contrivance, he observed some loose threads of the hempen string to stand erect, and to avoid one another, just as if they had been suspended on a common conductor. (Franklin)… immediately presented his knuckle to the key… he perceived a very evident electric spark."

The wet hemp string had conducted an electrical charge down to the iron

An illustration showing Ben Franklin's electrical experiment in June, 1752.

key, which is why a spark jumped to Franklin's knuckle when he tried to touch it. Franklin had proved that there is electricity in the atmosphere.

Don't try this in a real storm; lightning can kill. Franklin got lucky the day he conducted his experiment. If an actual lightning bolt had struck the kite, Franklin probably would have died that day. Instead, he went on to put his new-found knowledge to practical use. One of his most famous inventions is the lightning rod. It is a pole made of metal, like brass, that sits on top of houses or tall buildings. When lightning strikes, it hits the rod. The electrical charge is then carried down through a metal wire and safely into the ground, sparing the building from damage or fire. After more than 200 years, lightning rods are still in use today. Franklin considered it one of his most important inventions.

LIGHTNING INJURIES

ALTHOUGH IT IS EXTREMELY DANGEROUS, GETTING STRUCK BY lightning doesn't necessarily mean you'll die. Only 20 percent of people who are hit by lightning die right away. A lightning strike can deliver more than 300 kilovolts to the human body, but luckily it lasts a very short time, usually just a few milliseconds (millionths of a second).

The main cause of immediate death from a lightning strike is cardiopulmonary arrest—the heart and lungs simply stop working. If victims are revived, or manage to survive the strike without their hearts stopping, they will probably have other injuries to deal with. Lightning is very hot, and usually causes severe burns, both on the skin surface and deep inside the body. Internal organs are often severely injured.

Seventy percent of lightning victims who survive the strike will suffer long-term injury. Lightning is a nervous system injury—the brain and nerves that control bodily functions are often damaged. Victims often have short-term memory loss, are distracted easily, or are irritable. Many people are surprised at the victim's apparent personality change. They may also experience depression, and in extreme cases, may be prone to suicide.

Survivors often experience bad headaches. They may also suffer dizziness, nausea, and a ringing in the ears. These symptoms are similar to people who have suffered a concussion, a severe blow to the head. Fatigue and persistent, chronic pain are other common symptoms.

There is help for people coping with disabilities from lightning injuries. Most important is help from understanding family members, and doctors who are willing to listen and work with survivors.

A lightning storm over
Tucson, Arizona.

LIGHTNING SAFETY

MOST PEOPLE ARE STRUCK BY LIGHTNING BECAUSE THEY DON'T heed the warning signs. Most importantly, if a storm approaches, seek shelter immediately. The most dangerous place to be is outdoors. Many people are struck while at the beach, or golfing, or playing other outdoor games, or even just mowing the lawn. Finishing a game or a chore is not worth the risk of death or an injury that can last a lifetime.

Many people think they don't have to take shelter until it starts raining. Not true—most lightning victims are struck when it is not raining. In fact, lightning can strike many miles in advance of a storm cloud. These "bolts from the blue" are so common they kill many people without warning. At the first sound of thunder, even if you can't see the storm, seek shelter. And if you are swimming or boating, get to shore immediately.

A completely enclosed building, like a house or school, is the safest place to be. Open carports or patios are not safe. An automobile, with windows closed, will provide some shelter, but don't lean on the doors, or touch anything metal.

Once inside the shelter, stay away from electrical appliances, sockets, and plumbing, like bathtubs, showers, and sinks. In modern houses, a kind of plastic called polyvinyl chloride (PVC) has replaced metal pipes in indoor plumbing systems. Still, if you are not sure what kind of plumbing system your house has, stay away from plumbing.

Stay off the phone. If lightning hits your house, it will travel to every phone in your house. If you must make a call, use a cell phone or cordless phone.

A thunderstorm over Chicago, Illinois.

Better yet, wait out the storm before talking to someone on the telephone.

If you are stuck out in the wilderness or any wide-open area, stay away from tall objects like trees or telephone poles. Don't carry metal objects or other items that conduct electricity, like golf clubs, tennis rackets, or fishing rods. Get off your bicycle.

Don't stand in a group with other people—together you'll act like a big lightning rod. Stand at least several yards apart. If there is a shallow ditch nearby, get in it. Crouch down and make as

small and short a target as possible. Put your feet together and tuck your head down, covering your ears. If you're lucky, you won't get hit.

If someone is struck by lightning, first call 911. Then give first aid. It may be necessary to give CPR if the person has stopped breathing, or if their heart has stopped. If the victim is breathing and conscious, check for burns. People who have been struck by lightning do not carry an electrical charge, contrary to what some people think, so it is safe to examine them for injury.

FREQUENTLY ASKED QUESTIONS

Is it true that lightning never strikes the same place twice?

No. Lightning will seek the path of least resistance, which usually means the tallest and best conductor. It doesn't matter if the object has been struck before. The Empire State Building in New York City is struck by lightning about 25 times each year.

Can an airplane get hit by lightning?

Yes. Airplanes are frequently struck when flying through or close to thunderstorms. Luckily, lightning has not caused a plane to crash anywhere in the United States in more than 40 years. Most planes are made of aluminum, which is a very good conductor of electricity. Lightning flows along the airplane's skin and then back into the air. The airplane is not usually damaged. Sometimes a burn mark is left behind, or electronic equipment is damaged. It is extremely rare that a plane would be damaged enough to cause a major problem with flying.

There are rules that airplanes must have systems to keep sparks from igniting fuel lines or tanks. During the 1980s, NASA flew a research plane into 1,400 thunderstorms. Lightning hit the plane 700 times without damaging it.

Angry skies send lightning bolts toward a city.

Are cars safe from lightning because of their rubber tires?

No. Cars offer some protection against lightning strikes because of their metal shells, which dissipate the electricity. You should be safe as long as you don't lean on the doors or touch anything metal inside the car.

Will surge protectors keep electronics like computers and televisions safe?

No. Surge protectors only protect against small fluctuations in the electrical line coming from the power company. The powerful surge of electricity from a lightning strike will quickly fry any surge protector. However, there are products that can protect electronics from lightning strikes. A *lightning arrestor* is a special device that safely conducts a lightning surge to ground, sparing electronic devices from destruction.

Lightning strikes near a lighthouse.

How can I tell how far away a lightning strike is when it strikes?

You see a flash of lightning before you hear the thunder because light travels faster than the speed of sound. Light is so fast that it is almost instantaneous. Sound, on the other hand, only travels through the air at about 1,100 feet per second (335 meters per second) at ground level. At that speed, it takes a sound wave about five seconds to travel one mile (1.6 km). Count the number of seconds between a flash of lightning and the sound of thunder, then divide by five. This will tell you approximately how many miles you are from a lightning strike. For example, if the time between a flash of lightning and the sound of thunder is 10 seconds, this means the lightning struck about two miles (3.2 km) away. If you want to estimate how many kilometers away the lightning has struck, divide the seconds by three.

Lightning strikes in the Grand Canyon, Arizona. People who enjoy wilderness activities must be very careful of sudden thunderstorms.

Which state has the most number of lightning strikes?

Florida is the most dangerous state in the U.S. for lightning strikes. It is in a subtropical location, with many thunderstorms that roll across the land. Also, many people participate in outdoor sports in Florida, such as golfing or boating. Texas has the second most number of strikes.

What happens to fish when lightning strikes the water?

Many fish near the surface are killed. Water is a good conductor of electricity, making it dangerous to swim or boat during a thunderstorm. How far away and how deep the electricity penetrates depends on the power of the lightning stroke, but you could be in danger even if you are 100 feet (30 m) away.

GLOSSARY

AMPERAGE

Amperage is a basic measure of intensity of an electric current.

ATMOSPHERE

The air surrounding the earth, which is sometimes referred to as a gaseous envelope. The atmosphere extends about 621 miles (1,000 km) above the planet.

CARDIAC ARREST

Cardiac arrest occurs when the electrical activity of the heart is interrupted, which prevents it from pumping blood. Sometimes a severe electric shock, such as from a bolt of lightning, can cause a person to go into cardiac arrest.

CPR

CPR stands for cardiopulmonary resuscitation. It is an emergency medical technique used when a victim's heart and breathing have stopped. CPR is sometimes needed to revive victims of lightning strikes. It combines heart massage with mouth-to-mouth resuscitation. Almost anyone can learn to perform this life-saving technique when given the proper training.

ELECTRICAL DIFFERENTIAL

An electrical differential is simply a measure of the amount of energy a thundercloud contains. If there is a lot of electrical energy stored in the cloud, it has a high electrical differential.

INTER-CLOUD LIGHTNING

Lighting that jumps from one cloud to another is called inter-cloud lightning.

INTRA-CLOUD LIGHTNING

Lightning that is discharged within a cloud, shooting from pools of negative and positive electrons, is called intra-cloud lightning.

IONIZE

Ionized means to become electrically charged, like air in the presence of an intense electrical field. Air molecules under these conditions become separated into positive ions and negative electrons. Ionized air is also called plasma, and is very conductive to electricity.

STEPPED LEADER

A streamer of electricity that moves down from the negatively charged bottom of a thundercloud toward the ground, which is positively charged. Stepped leaders move in a short, step-like motion, creating channels through which electricity can flow.

VOLTAGE

Voltage measures the force, or pressure, that pushes electrons along an electrical circuit.

WEB SITES

WWW.ABDOPUB.COM

Would you like to learn more about lightning? Please visit www.abdopub.com to find up-to-date Web site links about lightning and other natural disasters. These links are routinely monitored and updated to provide the most current information available.

INDEX